HEROES AND WARRIORS

Nebuchadnezzar

SCOURGE OF ZION

MARK HEALY
Plates by RICHARD HOOK

Firebird Books

Also available in this series by the same author:

JOSHUA Conqueror of Canaan
KING DAVID Warlord of Israel
JUDAS MACCABEUS Rebel of Israel

For Martha and Benjamin

Acknowledgements

Most of the extracts from the *Babylonian Chronicle* are based upon the translation by D.J. Wiseman, whose invaluable contribution to any understanding of this major source is gratefully acknowledged. Other quotations are taken from *The New Jerusalem Bible* published by Darton Longman & Todd, whose translation and permission are gratefully acknowledged. For information on the military forces, the work of the Wargames Research Group is acknowledged and recommended.

First published in the UK 1989 by Firebird Books
P.O. Box 327, Poole, Dorset BH15 2RG

Copyright © 1989 Firebird Books Ltd
Text copyright © 1989 Mark Healy

Distributed in the United States by
Sterling Publishing Co, Inc,
Two Park Avenue, New York, NY 10016

Distributed in Australia by
Capricorn Link (Australia) Pty Ltd
PO Box 665, Lane Cove, NSW 2066

British Library Cataloguing in Publication Data

Healy, Mark
  Nebuchadnezzar.
  1. Nebuchadnezzar, *II, King of Babylonia, d. 562 B.C.*
  I. Title II. Series
  224'.5'0924

  ISBN 1 85314 009 0

Series editor Stuart Booth
Designed by Kathryn S.A. Booth
Typeset by Inforum Typesetting, Portsmouth
Monochrome origination by Castle Graphics, Frome
Colour separations by Kingfisher Facsimile
Colour printed by Barwell Colour Print (Midsomer Norton)
Printed and bound in Great Britain at The Bath Press

Nebuchadnezzar
SCOURGE OF ZION

A cuneiform inscription bearing the royal stamp of Nebuchadnezzar found on mud bricks throughout Babylonia.

Nebuchadnezzar, King of Babylon
patron of Esagila and Ezida
eldest son
of Nabopolassar, King of Babylon

THE EMPIRE OF NEBUCHADNEZZAR

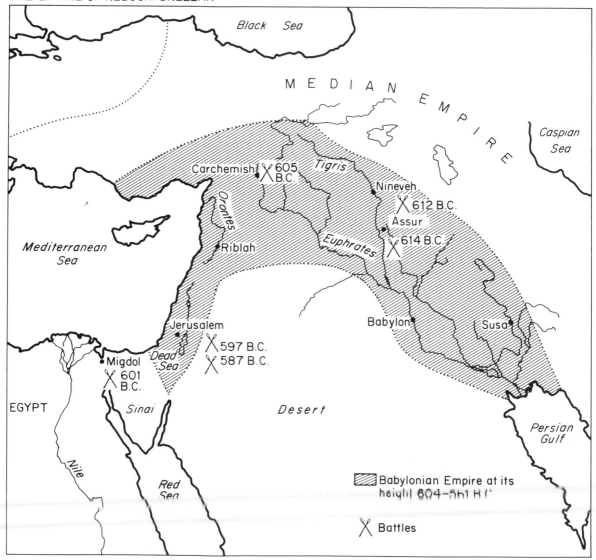

Great Babylon!
Was it not built by me as a royal residence,
By the force of my might
And for the majesty of my glory
                                        (Daniel 4:27–28)

What Manner of Man?

There are few names from the Ancient World more illustrious than that of Nebuchadnezzar. He was a great military leader, and a brilliant tactician and strategist. However it is for the rebuilding of one great city – Babylon – and for the destruction of another – Jerusalem in 587 B.C. that he is best remembered. The consequences of the latter event and the subsequent deportation of its population into exile are still with us even though the events occurred more than twenty-five centuries ago.

Out of the despair of the destruction of Jerusalem and of the great temple built by Solomon, the Jewish exiles in Babylon forged a new vision of their faith whose influence pervades the whole of western culture through the medium of the Judeo-Christian religious tradition.

Indeed, it is from the writings of the Jewish prophets – particularly of Jeremiah, Ezekiel and Daniel – that most people are familiar with the name of Nebuchadnezzar. Whilst the verdict is generally favourable there are aspects of his character and activities that leave some seeing him in a less than favourable light. The contemporary damning of imperialism has led to some labelling him as nothing more than a godless conqueror, bent only on territorial expansion at any cost.

However, it is important that one should not judge people out of their time and impose upon their milieu, values and beliefs that would be as alien to them, as theirs would be to us. Nebuchadnezzar lived in violent and brutal times; it is sometimes easy to forget when reading of sieges and battles that appear to us to be quite horrific, that for many people the world in which we live is in reality hardly less brutal.

It is difficult at this distance in time to analyse the personality of Nebuchadnezzar in the manner that is a necessary part of modern biography. One of the more significant omissions from the reports of his activities is the bombast and vainglory with which the Assyrian kings described their military deeds. Those Babylonian inscriptions that do exist, show him to have been a pious monarch who saw his activities arising out of a warrant from the gods. This was not new or even unique

– the kings of Assyria also claimed as much. What is interesting, however, is the degree to which he saw this divine vocation in terms of the dispensation of justice:

Without you, my lord, what exists? You establish the reputation of the king whom you love, whose name you pronounce and who pleases you. You make his reputation one of justice and set a straight forward course for him. I am the prince who obeys you, the creation of your hand. You begot me and entrusted me with the rule over all peoples.

This prayer was addressed to Marduk, the principal god of Nebuchadnezzar and Babylon. Certainly, the *Book of Daniel* speaks of the King as a man anxious about matters both moral and spiritual.

Like his father, he was an undoubted imperialist and pursued a policy of territorial expansion. Both were certainly influenced by the Assyrian imperial tradition and were no doubt seen in the same light as the earlier power by those who for so long had been under their domination. It is however to his life and career that we now turn.

Son of Nabopolassar

We do not know the exact year of Nebuchadnezzar's birth but it was certainly after 630 B.C. He was the eldest son of Nabopolassar and it is he who first mentions Nebuchadnezzar when he speaks of him as helping the early repair work on the great Ziggurat of Entemenanki in Babylon in 620 B.C.

The name of Nebuchadnezzar is more correctly rendered as Nabu-kudurri-usur, from the Akkadian, meaning: 'O Nabu, protect my offspring'.

Sources for this period of his life are sparse, but of this we are certain, he was born at a time of great events in the ancient Near East. The map of the 'world' was being redrawn, the old order was passing away and new empires were emerging. Instrumental in bringing about this great change was Nabopolassar, who in helping to bring about the collapse of Assyria, laid the foundations of the Neo-Babylonian empire, which was to rise to such great heights under his son.

Nabopolassar and Babylon

Nabopolassar seized power in Babylon in the period of turmoil that followed the death in 627 B.C. of Assurbanipal, the last great King of Assyria. The empire was on the verge of civil war as a consequence of a struggle for the succession to the Assyrian throne. Nabopolassar, in the best opportunistic fashion of his Chaldean forbears, marched on Babylon and seized the kingship for himself.

As to his origins, some have ascribed to him the leadership of the

The god Marduk or Bel (Lord) was the chief deity of Babylon. The splendid temple complex of Esagila, which was restored by Nebuchadnezzar, was dedicated to Marduk.

Chaldean tribe of the Bit Yakin, and thus the kingship of the 'Sea-Lands'. Such a position would suggest the recognition of his status by the Assyrians. Nabopolassar described himself as the 'son of a nobody', which does not imply humble origins as such, but rather tells us that he was not of the recognised ruling family of Babylon. His name, correctly rendered as Nabu-apal-usur, is pure Babylonian; but it suggests his birth place was the ancient city of Borsippa to the south of Babylon, whose god, Nabu or Nebo was worshipped there. Nevertheless, his ability to seize Babylon implies a degree of status and power that allowed his usurpation of the throne to be supported and accepted by the politically powerful elements within the city itself.

Over the centuries of Assyrian domination, Babylon had erupted repeatedly in rebellion; and Chaldean involvement was nearly always the catalyst. The Assyrian response had frequently been harsh and brutal. Twice in the preceding eighty years Babylon had suffered catastrophic sieges and the damage within the city was still visible at the time of Nabopolassar's accession.

Thus, it was with the 'blessings' of the gods of the land, voiced through the powerful temple priesthood and to the acclaim of the assembled nobility and tribal chiefs, that in November 626 B.C. Nabopolassar was crowned King of Akkad (Babylon). The dynasty he inaugurated is known either as the Chaldean or Neo-Babylonian. Under the aegis of himself and his successors, Babylon was transformed into the capital of the last great Mesopotamian empire, which after a brief glory lasting less than a century passed into the hands of Cyrus the Great of Persia in 539 B.C.

Alliance for Conquest
Nabopolassar's immediate concern on achieving power was to rebuild the Babylonian army in preparation for the contest of power with Assyria. The make-up and structure of the Neo-Babylonian army are examined later, but suffice it to say at this point that it must have drawn heavily on the Assyrian model for inspiration.

On the diplomatic front Nabopolassar began the search for allies. Of these efforts the most important were the overtures he made to Cyaxares, King of the Medes of Iran, who like Babylon had a long history of domination by and tribute payment to Assyria. Furthermore the Medes had just thrown off the yoke of the Scythians who had dominated Media for some twenty-five years. According to Herodotus, Cyaxares had re-organised his army, placing it on a new footing by separating the arms into distinctive units of lancers, cavalry and archers. Cyaxares had learned well the lessons of battle taught him by the Scythians and Assyrians and was now ready to turn this very formidable instrument of war against Nineveh itself, capital of Assyria. In the light of the subsequent role played by the Median armies against Assyria, it was their

An Akkadian infantryman of the Babylonian royal guard. Such soldiers attended Nebuchadnezzar when on campaign. Their uniform and equipment draw heavily on Assyrian types and designs.

7

participation that was in all likelihood the determining factor in Assyria's ultimate defeat. Although not formally bound by treaty, there is evidence to suggest that Babylon and Media began to act in concert on military operations directed at Assyria as early as 621 B.C.

Nabopolassar felt strong enough to first take the field against Assyria in 616. However, the next two years witnessed an indecisive march and countermarch by the rival armies as they jostled for advantage, their operations focussing on a line of Assyrian fortresses straddling the northern border of Babylonia.

It was at this time that a small Egyptian force made its appearance fighting alongside the Assyrians, heralding the appearance of yet another player in the drama that was unfolding on the Euphrates. This was only a token Egyptian force, but presaged the much greater involvement of this power in a conflict whose outcome was of great significance for her long-term interests in northern Syria and the lands of the Mediterranean seaboard.

The impasse was broken in 614 when Cyaxares invaded the heartland of Assyria itself. He had the intention of taking the imperial capital, but its massive defences defied the besiegers. Turning south, the fury of the Medes fell upon the city of Assur and in the words of the *Babylonian Chronicle*:

He (the Mede), says our Chronicle, made an attack upon the town . . . and the city wall he destroyed. He inflicted a terrible massacre upon the greater part of the people, plundering it and carrying off prisoners from it.

Nabopolassar and his army arrived too late to take part in the sack of the city, but amidst the smoking ruins of the former capital of the Empire, he and Cyaxares 'established mutual friendship and peace' and concluded the alliance that sealed the fate of the Assyrian Empire.

In personal terms, the most important outcome of the alliance between Babylon and Media was the marriage between Nebuchadnezzar and Amytis, the daughter of Cyaxares. Tradition relates that it was for her that he built that wonder of the Ancient World, the Hanging Gardens.

School of War

It seems reasonable to suppose that as he was growing to manhood, Nebuchadnezzar accompanied his father on his campaigns, observing at first hand the complexities of the art of war. The close co-operation that ensued between the Babylonian and Median armies would have exposed the young man to the different methods employed by the respective armies. The abilities he showed later on the battlefield must have their origin in this period. Certainly, the great events unfolding around him could scarcely have provided a more suitable training for a future reign that was spent almost annually in the field.

The storm god Adad worshipped by both Assyrians and Babylonians. The western gate in the 'new' city of Babylon was named for Adad.

Thus, his military career began whilst he was still a young man, and he was appointed to his first command in the year 610 B.C. As a military administrator in Babylonia, he raised troops to send to his father who was campaigning in the Harran area. The very fact that he was not with his father suggests that he was deemed responsible enough by Nabopolassar to deputise for the King in his absence. Although we cannot be certain of his age at this time, his preparation for his military responsibilities began many years before.

From an early age Nebuchadnezzar would have been conscious of the impact of war on Babylon. Virtually every year he would have watched his father, in his chariot, lead out the army through the Ishtar Gate to campaign in the north against the Assyrians. At court, which was constantly full of high ranking officers, he would overhear conversations of the battles fought on the frontier – and no doubt in deference to his status some of these soldiers would tell him of their experiences and relate anecdotes of life in the field.

As he grew older he began his own military training under the skilful eye of veterans appointed by his father. They would have developed his expertise with the sword, lance and bow. Others would have trained him in horsemanship and in the difficult and dangerous task of controlling a chariot team. As he matured, his training would have been expanded to cover such matters as strategy and tactics, siege warfare and logistics. He would have become acquainted with the different units that made up the Babylonian army, learning to understand their strengths and weaknesses. As the war against Assyria entered its final phase it seems likely that his father would have included him in any discussions in which political and military strategy were discussed with his senior officers. Very probably he joined his father on campaign, as was suggested earlier, and was in all likelihood present at the fall of Assur and

Chaldean infantry like these provided the bulk of the troops fielded by the Babylonian armies. Their body protection was minimal and they were lightly armed, with the compound bow their main weapon. Spears and wicker shields enabled these soldiers to close in upon their enemy.

Nineveh. His marriage to Cyaxares' daughter Amytis laid the foundation of the initially good relationship that existed between Media and himself when he was King. His first-hand observations of the Median armies in action must have had some effect on his handling of Babylonian troops who under his father were never noted for their military prowess. The very fact that Nebuchadnezzar, within a few short months of being appointed its commander-in-chief, could take the Babylonian army and destroy the Egyptian army suggests that he possessed a remarkable military talent.

In 607–606, having been designated Crown Prince, he commanded an army with his father in northern Assyria. Nabopolassar returned to Babylon after a month and left the young Crown Prince in charge of the army. He undertook independent operations against rebellious hill tribesmen, a campaign of four months, which culminated in the destruction and looting of a city. Thereafter he was constantly engaged in military operations to help his father. By 605 B.C., the Babylonian monarch's declining health and the growing proof of Nebuchadnezzar's military abilities led to Nabopolassar handing over the army to his son. With that army Nebuchadnezzar was to create in less than twenty years an empire that at its height was larger than that of Assyria under Assurbanipal. Clearly, in the hands of Nebuchadnezzar it became a formidable instrument of power and is deserving of a closer study.

Forces of Battle

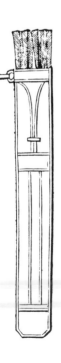

Whilst no Babylonian counterpart exists of the wall reliefs from the palaces of the Assyrian kings, it is likely the Neo-Babylonian armies of Nebuchadnezzar drew heavily on the organisation, types of equipment and tactics employed by the Assyrian army at the time of Assurbanipal. Also, the Babylonians had contact with the armies of Elam, often in alliance with them against Assyria, and affecting the tactics and make-up of aspects of the Neo-Babylonian forces. Additionally, Nebuchadnezzar's own observations and experience of Median military methods had some influence on the way his forces evolved.

The Babylonian Army

The Babylonian army of Nebuchadnezzar was almost certainly composed of two principal elements. The core of the fighting force was made up of professional soldiers who provided the royal guard, the chariotry, the heavy cavalry and the engineer troops.

Whilst most of the soldiers were native Babylonians (Akkadian), Nebuchadnezzar certainly made use of Greek mercenary troops, but not on the scale of his Egyptian opponents. Elite units were also drawn from the Chaldean tribes of the 'Sea-Lands' and it is entirely conceivable that soldiers from the tribe of the Bit Yakin formed part of the King's personal bodyguard. Such then were the units that made up the standing army and which were available for garrison duties in the empire.

In the campaigning season the standing army was joined by the second component, tribal levies called to the 'colours' by the King. Most of these troops were Chaldean and were organised in tribal units. Unlike the units of the standing army they were very lightly equipped and in battle provided the bulk of the forces. Whilst they were important, it was on the units of the standing army that Nebuchadnezzar depended to gain victory. It is significant that in the one 'detailed' reference to a major battle in the *Babylonian Chronicle*, that at Migdol in 601 B.C., it was the very heavy losses amongst the cavalry and chariotry that brought about a Babylonian withdrawal from Egypt. Without those elements of the army, it was impossible for Nebuchadnezzar to bring a decisive end to the campaign.

Battlefield Tactics

In the light of observations of the make-up of the Babylonian army, the line-up on the field of battle would look as follows:

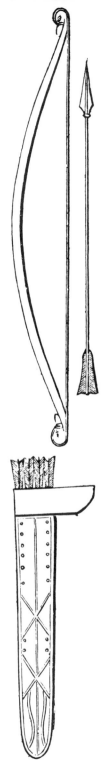

HEAVY CHARIOTS	CHALDEAN LEVIES Mass archers with light infantry armed with spears/shields	HEAVY CHARIOTS
CAVALRY		CAVALRY

ROYAL GUARD
More heavily
armoured infantry

KING (?)

At the beginning of the battle, long-range fire would be opened on the enemy lines by the massed archers of the tribal levies. It is possible that this fire might have been sustained for some considerable time until the King or the commanding officer perceived some wavering in the enemy lines. It would have been directed at the foot soldiers, but more particularly at the enemy's chariot forces and cavalry. At a given signal, the heavy four-horsed chariots would begin their charge, the archer(s) on board firing on the move. Shield bearers on the chariots would attempt

Amongst many quivers used with bows by the Babylonian army (above and opposite), many would have shown the strong influence of Assyrian design.

11

A heavy, four-horsed chariot similar to the type employed by the Babylonians as the main shock weapon in their battles. Although this is a late Assyrian model, from the reign of Assur-banipal, Babylonian chariots looked little different.

to protect the chariot crew from the enemy counter-fire. The effect of the chariot was both physical (little could stop such a heavy vehicle at full tilt and any infantry caught in its path would be run down) and psychological (the sight of charging massed chariots unnerving the enemy and causing them to flee in panic).

The cavalry would then follow up to exploit the gaps created in the enemy lines, and if possible turn the flanks in an encircling movement. If the enemy began a full-scale retreat, then their task was to harry, pursue and ride down the escaping soldiers.

Once the chariots and cavalry were engaged the central infantry would advance and close with the opposition. A large number of the light troops were equipped with spears, swords and large wicker shields to enable them to engage in close combat.

Such a battle would soon become a very bloody mêlée with little quarter being given by either side. Some sense of the sheer ferocity of the ancient battlefield can be gained by considering a report by the Assyrian king Sennacherib when he fought against a combined Elamite and Chaldean-Babylonian army in 691 B.C.:

I rushed upon the enemy like the approach of a hurricane . . . I put them to rout and turned them back. I transfixed the troops of the enemy with javelins and arrows. Humban undasha, the commander-in-chief of the King of Elam, together with his nobles . . . I cut their throats like sheep . . . My prancing steeds, trained to harness, plunged into their welling blood as into a river; the wheels of my battle chariot were bespattered with blood and filth. I filled the plain with the corpses of their warriors like herbage . . . There were chariots with their horses, whose riders had been slain as they came into the fierce battle, so that they were loose by themselves; those horses kept going back and forth all over the place to a distance of two double hours . . . As to the sheikhs of the Chaldeans, panic from my onslaught overwhelmed them like a demon. They abandoned their tents and fled for their lives, crushing the corpses of their troops as they went . . . In their terror they passed scalding urine and voided their excrement into their chariots.

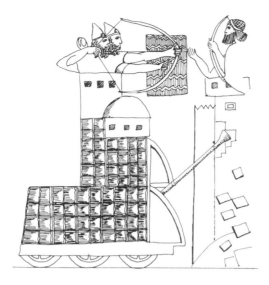

Siege Warfare

Throughout the reign of Nebuchadnezzar the Babylonian army was required to undertake a large number of sieges.

Siege warfare was the most complex of operations for an army to undertake in ancient times. Certainly the Babylonian army was provided with a siege train which accompanied the advance of the main army when on campaign. As in the case of the Assyrian examples, much of the material to build the siege towers would have been carried on wagons in parts broken down for re-assembly where needed, although there are a number of texts that also imply that the fully assembled siege towers were actually manhandled across considerable distances ready for use. The *Babylonian Chronicle* refers to a campaign in 603-602 B.C., the second year of Nebuchadnezzar's reign, to some point in the west which is assumed to refer to Hatti-Land in which a town (city) was laid siege to by bringing the siege towers across the mountains.

Whilst the major powers could contest with each other on the battlefield, smaller powers such as Judah, did not have the resources to field large armies to stave off predatory imperial powers. Consequently, they applied themselves to creating highly effective defences around their major cities that would frustrate, and hopefully defeat, the attempts of besieging forces to conquer them. As defences became more effective, the main strategy for taking a fortified city was to allow starvation and disease to take its toll on the people within the walls. Earthworks would be thrown up around the city to enclose the populace and the besieging army would then wait until the moment was deemed appropriate to finally storm the walls at their weakest point.

A number of sources speak of the Babylonian armies bringing large siege towers into action. Alas, we have no direct renderings of these engines although it is extremely likely that they were very similar to the larger Assyrian types. The use of these siege towers would have covered the operations of battering rams and mining operations designed to breach the walls. The problems of siege warfare can be gauged by the time taken to capture Jerusalem and the Phoenician city of Tyre. Jerusalem was under siege for two years, whereas Tyre tied down Babylonian troops for some thirteen years. (Although it has to be said that Tyre raised particular problems, being very difficult to invest properly by virtue of its isolation from the mainland; and a sheltered harbour allowed it to be supplied by vessels of its own fleet and that of Egypt.)

The Egyptian Army

In many ways the Egyptian army fielded by Necho II at Carchemish operated in a manner almost identical to that of the Babylonian forces opposing them. The traditional, central disposition of infantry with the chariots on the wings supported by cavalry would have led to tactics very similar to those of the Babylonians. However, the power of the Babylonian chariotry may well have been greater by virtue of the larger size of the chariot and crew, with a correspondingly greater effectiveness in the charge. A further difference is that the Egyptian infantry were far better organised for close order fighting than were those of Babylon, with fewer archers.

The impact of the heavily armoured and armed *haw-nebu* or 'new foreigner' from Asia Minor had a profound effect on the Egyptian army in the Saite period. The presence of these Greek mercenaries at Carchemish has been confirmed by the discovery by archaeologists of a Greek greave and bronze shield with a gorgon's head, amidst the arrow-riddled remains of a building containing a number of Egyptian items, some bearing the cartouche of Necho II. Other Greek mercenaries served with the Judaean army; evidence of their presence has been found at Mesad Hashavyahu, thought to have been a Greek mercenary settlement.

Nebuchadnezzar's chariots carried a crew of four. Two shield bearers provided cover for the driver and archer. Thus, the chariot could be used as a fighting platform, advancing and withdrawing from enemy lines.

14

The Fall of Nineveh

Two years after Nebuchadnezzar's marriage, a combined Babylonian and Median army attacked Nineveh itself. The *Babylonian Chronicle* describes the final demise of the great city:

From the month of Sivan to the month of Ab three battles were fought. They made a strong attack on the citadel and in the month of Ab the city was taken and a great defeat inflicted on the people and their chiefs. On that same day Sin-shar-ishkun, the Assyrian king, perished in the flames. They carried off much spoil from the city and temple area and turned the city into a ruin mound and heap of debris.

The speed with which the city fell is surprising, lending credence to traditions found in Greek and Biblical sources that an entrance into the city was effected by diverting the waters of a river, probably the Khosr, against the walls. These then washed away some of the city's powerful defences.

For nearly three hundred years Assyria had dominated the Fertile Crescent, its seemingly invincible armies ranging in their incessant campaigns from Elam and the Persian Gulf in the east to Egypt in the west. The great cities of Assyria had grown fabulously wealthy from the booty and tribute from the lands over which she held sway. Few had escaped their power and their record of cruelty had endeared them to none. Thus, with Nineveh's destruction, there were none to mourn Assyria's passing.

One of the very few depictions of the soldiers available to us from the Neo-Babylonian period. Detail is sparse, but the soldier on the left of the middle frame is clearly employing a compound bow, one of the major weapons of the troops in Nebuchadnezzar's army.

The significance of the event was not lost on Nabopolassar. In the sweetness of victory, he contemplated the final triumph of Babylon over Nineveh:

I slaughtered the land of Subarum (Assyria), I turned the hostile land into heaps and ruins. The Assyrian, who since distant days had ruled over all peoples, and with his heavy yoke had brought injury to the people of the Land, his feet from Akkad I turned back, his yoke I threw off.

The rump of the Assyrian army retreated westwards to the city of Harran to await the arrival of assistance from their Egyptian allies. Thus, it was in Harran that one Assur-uballit, a junior member of the royal family, was crowned as the last King of Assyria.

As the pitiful remnants of the Assyrian army posed no further threat, the victorious allies parted. Cyaxares returned to his homeland, his army weighed down with booty and prisoners by the thousands destined for the slave markets of Media. Nabopolassar, intent on exploiting the collapse of Assyrian power, moved quickly to occupy as many of their former lands as he could.

Battle of Harran and Aftermath

The next two years were spent in the lands of the middle Euphrates in operations designed to enforce Babylonian control on an area that had for centuries been part of Assyria. It was a two-year breathing space that allowed Assur-uballit in Harran to regroup his forces and bolster his army with reinforcements from Egypt.

In 610 the Medes and the Babylonians moved against Harran. In the face of overwhelmingly superior forces:

Assur-uballit and the army of Egypt which had come to help him, the fear of the enemy fell on them, they abandoned the city and crossed the river Euphrates. The Babylonian king reached Harran . . . captured the city they carried off much spoil from the city and temple.

The Médes withdrew – once again satisfied with the booty from the sacked city as the price of their exertions – to establish their own empire in Armenia and Asia Minor. The sack and occupation of Harran placed the Babylonian forces in a strong position. As they were poised to advance into Syria, a land long coveted by the great powers of the Fertile Crescent for its strategic position and its great economic wealth, other forces were about to enter the game.

Carchemish and Coronation

It was the news of the defeat at Harran that prompted the new Pharaoh of Egypt, Necho II (610–595 B.C.) to call out the whole of his army and march northwards to support the remnants of Assur-uballit's forces.

Nebuchadnezzar was given command of the Babylonian army in 605 B.C. He defeated the Egyptians under Necho II in the bloody battle of Carchemish, placing Judah under Babylonian power.

Necho successfully effected a junction with the forces of the Assyrian King at Carchemish, but not before defeating the army of Josiah, King of Judah at Megiddo. The motives of Josiah in seeking battle with the Egyptians are unclear. Certainly, the very brief account does little to enlighten us:

Pharaoh Necho king of Egypt was advancing to meet the king of Assyria at the river Euphrates, and king Josiah went to intercept him; but Necho killed him at Megiddo in the first encounter.

(2 Kings 24:29)

Amidst the possible answers that have been offered, a most credible explanation lies in a diplomatic overture by Nabopolassar to Josiah, with some political inducement for him to take the field and attempt to bar the passage of the Egyptian army. Nevertheless, Megiddo was but a diversion. The main task of what was an overwhelming Egyptian army in northern Syria was to block the Babylonian drive towards the Mediterranean.

End of Empire

The initial success could not be sustained and the force withdrew to Carchemish. The name of Assur–uballit disappears hereafter from the *Chronicle* and with his demise the last traces of the Assyrian empire disappeared forever. With their ally finally destroyed, the Egyptian effort lay subsequently in the defeat of a major Babylonian offensive which was designed to take the rest of Syria, and with its fall the whole of the Mediterranean seaboard including Palestine.

Such a task seemed at first possible. The three years following the second battle of Harran saw a jostling for military advantage by both armies, with neither gaining the upper hand. It was the appointment of the Crown Prince, Nebuchadnezzar, to the command of the army in Syria in 605 B.C. that ended the stalemate. Within a few short months he had shattered the Egyptian army in a battle so decisive that according to the Bible:

The king of Egypt did not leave his own country again, because the king of Babylon had conquered everywhere belonging to the king of Egypt from the Torrent of Egypt to the river Euphrates.

(2 Kings 24:7)

The apprenticeship in arms of the young Nebuchadnezzar provides considerable insight into the truly decisive nature of the battle. Whilst the armies themselves were important it was the qualitative difference brought to the battlefield by the generalship of Nebuchadnezzar himself that was the deciding factor.

Victory

The battle of Carchemish can truly be described as one of the decisive battles of the Ancient World. Yet as with many other specific incidents

In November 598 B.C. Nebuchadnezzar mustered his army and led them forth through the Ishtar Gate of Babylon to campaign in the 'Hatti' land – a familiar event – and to chastise the rebel Judah.

and events of the period, we lack the direct evidence and sources that allow a detailed account of the momentous clash of arms. Nevertheless, it is possible to gain a general idea as to the course of events.

Carchemish was established by Necho II as the major Egyptian garrison city in Syria. It was well placed to allow movement to and from Egypt, as well as offering a good central base for the war of manoeuvre being undertaken by the Pharaoh and the Babylonian King as the latter attempted to cut the Egyptian supply lines on the upper Euphrates. Two attempts, in 606 B.C., by Nabopolassar to establish garrisons to the north and south of Carchemish had been seen off by the Egyptians. There thus existed a situation of stalemate when in 605 B.C. Nabopolassar handed over control of the army to his son and heir designate.

In the light of the indecision of the previous year it is likely that it was the speed of Nebuchadnezzar's advance that forced the battle. Certainly the strategy he adopted was in essence little different to that of his father – to cut off the Egyptian supply lines. Nebuchadnezzar took his army across the Euphrates to the west bank and attacked Carchemish directly. Perhaps catching the Egyptians unprepared for a major engagement, he was able to force the decisive battle that was necessary to bring about a decision in Syria.

The outcome was a bloody confrontation in which both sides suffered heavy losses: 'for warrior has stumbled against warrior, and both have fallen down together.'

The Egyptian line broke under the ferocity of the Babylonian attack. The *Babylonian Chronicle* speaks of the Crown Prince 'smashing them out of existence'. The remnants of the Egyptian army abandoned the battlefield and fled in headlong retreat to the south. Nebuchadnezzar instigated a major pursuit and the retreat turned into a rout, with the *Chronicle* claiming:

A mounted lancer of the type found in the Assyrian armies of the late seventh century B.C. Babylonian cavalry would have looked very similar. The horse is protected by felt armour, whilst the trooper is liberally equipped with weapons. Apart from the lance, he carries a composite bow and sword. The overarm carriage of the lance shows that it was used as a thrusting weapon.

As for the remnant of the Egyptian army which had escaped from the defeat so hastily that no weapon touched them, the Babylonian army overwhelmed them and defeated them in the district of Hamath, so that not a single man escaped to his own country.

The consequence of the battle was quite clear:

At that time Nebuchadnezzar conquered the whole land of Hatti.

Nebuchadnezzar was probably at Riblah, which was to become the main Babylonian garrison in southern Syria and the base for his future operations in the west, when the news of his father's death reached him:

For twenty one years Nabopolassar had been king of Babylonia. On the eighth of Ab he died; in the month of Elul Nebuchadnezzar returned to Babylon.

According to Berosus, the third century Babylonian priest and historian:

the prisoners . . . Jews, Phoenicians, Syrians and those of Egyptian nationality were consigned to some of Nebuchadnezzar's friends, with orders to conduct them to Babylonia along with the heavy troops and the rest of the spoils; while he himself, with a small escort, pushed across the desert to Babylon.

Nebuchadnezzar reached Babylon and on 'the first day of Elul' – 6th September 605 B.C. – he sat on the royal throne that he was to occupy for forty-two years. There were no problems in the city and the accession passed smoothly to him.

At the beginning of his accession year he celebrated the New Year Festival in Babylon. The high point of the celebration occurred when the King had 'taken the hand of Bel Marduk and the son of Bel to lead them

A view of Babylon's remains from the north of the famous Procession Street, clearly showing the reconstruction work being undertaken by the Iraqi Department of Antiquities. This 'street' stretched from the Ishtar Gate to the middle of the city, and along it, at the time of the New Year Festival, would have passed the images of Marduk and the other gods on their way to the Akitu House, beyond the inner city walls. The Festival was a significant event in the city's religious calendar.

out in the procession'. For Nebuchadnezzar, the event was of immense significance for it was from the hand of Marduk – 'his lord' – that the new King claimed the grant of universal kingship along with the request petitioned in prayer that he: 'have no opponent from horizon to sky'.

Prophets and Kings

It is a measure of Nebuchadnezzar's authority in Babylon itself that within a very short time of his coronation he returned to Syria–Lebanon. From his base of operations at Riblah he directed his armies in a wide-ranging campaign designed to pacify the area and bring it to heel:

In the accession year Nebuchadnezzar went back to Hatti-land and marched victoriously through it until the month of Sebat. In the month of Sebat he took the heavy tribute of the Hatti-land back to Babylon.

Riches of Conquest

Judaean spearman with a typical heavy leather shield, strengthened with bronze around the rim and boss. Although the soldier shown here was in the service of the Assyrian King Sennacherib, Judean troops at the time of Nebuchadnezzar would have looked little different.

For nearly two millennia the lands of Syria and the Lebanon had witnessed the tramp of foreign soldiers as in their turn Egyptian, Hittite, Assyrian and now Babylonian armies sought to control the immense mineral and commercial wealth of the area to their own advantage. From the mountains of the Lebanon came the mighty cedars and cypresses whose trunks were used by many of the monarchs of the Fertile Crescent to adorn their palaces and temples. Indeed, Nebuchadnezzar tells us in great detail (in an inscription cut into a rock face in the valley of Brissa) of a campaign directed towards securing access to and control of the cedars of the Lebanon:

At that time Mount Lebanon, the (cedar) mountain, luxuriant forest of Marduk, sweet scented . . . over which an enemy alien held sway and was taking away its produce. Its population were scattered and had taken refuge in distant places. In the strength of Nabu and Marduk my lords, I drew up (my troops) in an array for battle against Lebanon to (take it). I cleared out its enemy on the heights and in the lowlands I made glad the hearts of the land. I gathered together its scattered population and brought them back to their place. A thing which no former king had done (that is) I broke up the towering mountains, I ground the limestone, and thus I opened up approaches and made a straight way for the cedars. I made the Arakhtu canal carry as though they were reeds, the hardy, tall, stout cedars, of surpassing quality and impressively black of aspect, solid products of mount Lebanon, to Marduk my king.

Other produce of the mountains included gold, silver, copper and precious stones. Into Tyre and Sidon, the great ports of Phoenicia, flowed the 'yield of the sea', for the commerce of the Mediterranean lands had for many centuries been brought into the near east in Phoenician vessels. Many of the luxury goods on which the Assyrians had depended, and which the Babylonians now wished for themselves, came from these Levantine ports. The goods and the taxes levied upon them now belonged to Nebuchadnezzar by right of conquest.

The economic importance of the area was further enhanced by virtue of it being the confluence of a number of vital trade routes. Of these, the most important were those from the south, whose passage through Palestine made their dislocation unacceptable to the Babylonians. Whilst Egyptian interests in the area, which were almost identical to those of Babylon, had received a reversal at the battle of Carchemish, her continued ambitions in Syria–Lebanon resulted in efforts to stir up trouble in areas now under Babylonian domination. Neither Phoenicia, Philistia nor Judah, who had for many decades each been vassals of Assyria, had any desire to pay tribute to another Mesopotamian power so soon after the fall of Nineveh, an event which had raised their hopes of freedom and independence.

Struggle in Judah

In the year following his coronation, Nebuchadnezzar marched un-opposed into Palestine. Following the Babylonian siege of the Philistine city of Ashkelon, Jehoiakim, King of Judah submitted to Nebuchadnez-zar and became his vassal. The tribute levied on Judah included articles and vessels from the great temple in Jerusalem and according to the *Book of Daniel*: 'These he took away to Shinar (Babylon), putting the vessels into the treasury of his own gods'.

The seeming invincibility of the arms of the Babylonian monarch had thus temporarily forced the people of Judah to reconcile themselves to paying tribute to the new Mesopotamian power. It was a bitter pill to have to swallow.

Such was the backdrop against which a dramatic confrontation was taking place in Judah itself. At stake was the continued survival of the throne of David and at issue was the way Judah should conduct itself in the face of the changed international situation. The struggle is personi-fied in the perspectives of the two principal antagonists, whose perspec-tives deserve examination if one is to understand the significance of the subsequent events.

Who Speaks for Yahweh?

When in 609 B.C. the body of the thirty-nine year old Josiah was returned to Jerusalem for burial, his younger son Jehoahaz was chosen to succeed him. However, the wishes of the people of Judah did not accord with those of the Pharaoh of Egypt. Upon presenting himself to Necho II at Riblah, to acknowledge the Egyptian as Judah's overlord, the Pharaoh had him placed in chains and deprived Jehoahaz of his crown.

This act was sufficient to show that Judah was still the vassal of the Pharaoh of Egypt and that in appointing a king for themselves, the people of Judah had presumed for themselves a right that remained a preserve of their overlord. The new King, Jehoiakim, together with the majority of the political establishment of Judah, remained loyal to

Judean archers, at the time of Nebuchadnezzar's invasion would have been equipped very similarly to this earlier archer from Judah, a captive in the service of Sennacherib, the Assyrian king.

21

Egypt. It was only when the reality of Babylonian power was made manifest with the destruction of Ashkelon that Jehoiakim reluctantly transferred his loyalty to Nebuchadnezzar. The King of Judah paid tribute to Nebuchadnezzar for only three years before openly rebelling against his Babylonian overlord. That in itself is testimony that his submission was but an expedient, pending what he and many others in Judah believed to be the imminent and inevitable resurgence of the fortunes of Egypt in Palestine.

Optimism for the future of Judah, under the benevolent hegemony of the great southern power, was in marked contrast to the message of one Jeremiah, son of Hilkiah, a prophet of Yahweh, the God of the Jews, who had already pronounced the sentence of doom on the whole nation:

So . . . this is what Yahweh Sabaoth says, 'Since you have not listened to my words, I shall send for all the families of the north (Yahweh declares, that is for Nebuchadnezzar king of Babylon, my servant) and bring them down on this country and its inhabitants (and on all the surrounding nations); I shall curse them with utter destruction and make them an object of horror, of scorn, and ruin them for ever. From them I shall banish the shouts of rejoicing and mirth, the voices of bridegroom and bride, the sound of the handmill and the light of the lamp; and this whole country will be reduced to ruin and desolation, and these nations will be enslaved to the king of Babylon for seventy years.'

(Jeremiah 25:8–12)

Such, in essence, was the message read to the Temple priesthood by Baruch, a scribe employed by Jeremiah, as the prophet himself was banned from preaching within the Temple precincts. It is not surprising that the message generated alarm, and to many listening sounded like treason. Consequently, Baruch and his master were advised to go into hiding, while the scroll itself was taken before the King and read to him.

A temple official by the name of Jehudi had been ordered by the King to appear before him and read the text of Jeremiah's scroll. The winter that year was undoubtedly cold, for Jehoiakim was warming himself within the palace in front of a blazing brazier when Jehudi arrived. What follows gives us an insight into the personality of Jehoiakim:

Each time Jehudi had read three or four columns, the king cut them off with a scribe's knife and threw them into the fire in the brazier until the whole scroll had been burnt in the brazier fire. But in spite of hearing all these words, neither king nor any of the courtiers took alarm or tore their clothes, and although Elnathan and Delaiah and Gemariah had urged the king not to burn the scroll he would not listen to them.

(Jeremiah 36:23–26)

As the temple officials had feared, Jehoiakim ordered the arrest of Jeremiah. But he and Baruch could not be found and upon hearing of the destruction of the first scroll, Jeremiah had dictated another. Nothing illustrates the depth of the antipathy that existed between the two men better than Jehoiakim's treatment of the scroll. Clearly, in his calm and deliberated dismissal he regarded its contents as the rantings of a madman. The prophets had always had uncertain relationships with the kings whom they addressed, but Jehoiakim's destruction of the scroll shows the degree to which he believed the words of Jeremiah to be an utter irrelevancy to Judah's situation.

In his new scroll, Jeremiah revealed the depth of his loathing for the man who occupied the throne of David. He saw in Jehoiakim's dismissal of the contents of the scroll – the word of Yahweh – evidence of the very sin of arrogance which would doom Judah.

A Chosen People

At the heart of the Jewish tradition – thereafter inherited and developed by Christianity in a modified and distinct manner – is a conviction that there exists a special relationship between the Jews and the one true God. Specifically, it is an article of the Jewish faith that in about the thirteenth century B.C. their ancestors were liberated from slavery in Egypt. The significance of the Exodus from Egypt lay in the conviction that Yahweh had intervened decisively in history in order to bring about an event that could not have occurred if left to human devices.

In the desert of the Sinai, a more formal relationship was established between Yahweh and the Hebrew tribes when they freely entered into a legal and binding agreement called a covenant. The terms of the covenant, as communicated through Moses, required that the Hebrew tribes agreed to live by Yahweh's commandments. In return, they would be given a land of their own. As long as the Commandments of Yahweh were upheld, then Yahweh would ensure that his bounty and beneficence were enjoyed by his chosen people; but in the event of the people forsaking their obligations under the covenant, He would punish them.

The task laid upon the prophets throughout the period of the Hebrew kingdoms was to speak out for Yahweh in the face of the people's breaking of the Commandments. Always their denunciation of the backsliding of the chosen people ended with a promise of Yahweh's punishment in a manner that saw the emergence of a very different explanation of historical events. Yahweh, as the one true God, was also the Lord of history and thus able to call on the nations of all lands to effect his purpose. To the prophets, there was a rationale to international affairs that transcended the mundane explanation of events as being the mere product of the policies of the great powers.

Thus, the mighty nations of the ancient near east became the unwitting pawns whereby Yahweh punished his chosen people. The prophet Isaiah had seen even Assyrian imperialism as part of the divine purpose; other prophets of Judah saw in the armies of Babylon and in the person of Nebuchadnezzar the latest instrument of Yahweh's wrath against his people.

Therefore, Jeremiah became the most prominent voice against those who put their trust in Egypt. For him, the submission of Judah to Babylon was inevitable, for Nebuchadnezzar was the chosen instrument of Yahweh. So, to entertain escape from the domination of the Mesopotamian monarch was inviting the destruction that he had already foreseen as inevitable. Indeed, Jeremiah poured scorn on those who naively believed that Yahweh would not countenance the destruction of Jerusalem simply because the great temple built by Solomon was located there.

Jehoiakim ignored the words of Jeremiah and having paid tribute to Nebuchadnezzar for only three years, in 600 B.C. he actually withheld payment to his overlord. That made him legally in breach of his submission to the King of Babylon, and technically in a state of rebellion against Nebuchadnezzar. Such an action was bound to bring forth a harsh military response.

What could possibly have motivated such an irresponsible and potentially suicidal action? The answer lies outside of Judah itself, on the wider stage of the confrontation between Babylon and Egypt.

War with Egypt

In the fourth year of his reign, Nebuchadnezzar called up his army and, as in previous years, marched to 'the Hatti-land'. His task was to replenish the military garrisons with new troops and supplies, and generally oversee the security situation on the southern border with Egypt.

From his forward base at Riblah, the main Babylonian garrison in southern Syria, he held court. It was to Riblah that his vassals travelled with their annual tributes, continuing tokens of their submission to him. However, it was not only gold, silver and other valuables that he demanded from them. Military intelligence of Egyptian intentions in southern Palestine was vital to the Babylonian capacity to maintain control of the area. Thus, Nebuchadnezzar had charged each vassal, including Jehoiakim, in his loyalty oath to 'keep the country for him and attempt no uprising nor show friendliness to the Egyptians'. No doubt part of this requirement was to forward to the military commanders in Syria any intelligence of Egyptian actions and intentions in the area. One must also presume that, like the Assyrians, Nebuchadnezzar had a well-developed system of spies reporting regularly. Collation of these reports would thus have allowed him to keep his eye on the Egyptians and on his vassals as well.

In addition, Nebuchadnezzar most likely anticipated trouble in the area. Given that Jehoiakim was a protégé of Necho II, and had been dealt with harshly as a consequence by Nebuchadnezzar in 604 B.C., the Babylonians more than half expected the Judaean monarch to rebel if the situation in Palestine should turn in Egypt's favour. The desire to maintain control in southern Palestine, and to ensure the loyalty of his vassals in the area, meant that Nebuchadnezzar would have to take rapid

and decisive action in the face of Egyptian attempts to destabilize the area.

Whether this was perceived to be precisely the case by the Babylonian King late in 601 B.C. is uncertain. Nevertheless, after raising his army to full strength – which possibly included calling upon the soldiers of his vassals, including a very reluctant Jehoiakim – Nebuchadnezzar marched south to begin a major military operation interpreted by some commentators as a full-scale invasion of Egypt.

Victory at Migdol

Nebuchadnezzar may well have concluded that an invasion of Egypt was the only solution that in the longer term would keep Palestine secure. Whatever his motivation, his invasion resulted in the largest and bloodiest battle since Carchemish.

Identifying the exact site of this battle is problematic. Some authorities speak of the Gaza plain. Alternatively, Herodotus of Halicarnassus, the Greek historian, speaks of King Necos (Necho II) attacking the Syrians (Babylonians) by land and defeating them at Magdolus (or Migdol), which is in Egypt itself on the eastern edge of the Nile delta and identified as the site of Tell el-Heir. In the words of the *Babylonian Chronicle:*

In the month of Kislev he took the lead of his army and marched toward Egypt. The king of Egypt heard of it and sent out his army; they clashed in an open battle and inflicted heavy losses on each other. The king of Akkad and his army turned back and returned to Babylon

It is however the next part of that text that provides a real insight into the nature of the damage suffered in the battle by the Babylonian army:

In the fifth year (600–599 B.C.) the King of Akkad stayed in his own land and gathered his chariots and horses in great numbers.

The inference is clear; Nebuchadnezzar suffered very heavy losses in the mobile units of his army to such a degree that any further advance into Egypt was no longer possible. The *Chronicle* speaks of 'an open battle' and undoubtedly the mobile forces of cavalry and chariotry on either side played a very major part in the battle. Headlong clashes of large numbers of cavalry and chariots, each attempting to turn the other's open flank, would have resulted in the very heavy losses spoken of. In the years since the conflict at Carchemish, Necho II had rebuilt his army and was now employing many more heavily-armoured Greek mercenary troops. The clash, on the very borders of Egypt itself, would have imparted a sense of resolve that would have made the Pharaoh's army fight with a fervour that compensated for the reputation of invincibility which preceded Nebuchadnezzar's army in the field. The result was probably a draw.

However, Migdol was no Carchemish. The headlong flight of the Egyptian troops following that battle in northern Syria some six years before finds no parallel here. The ruthless and relentless pursuit by the Babylonian army was not repeated; there seems to have been no attempt by the Egyptian forces to harry the retreating Babylonians.

Abandoning the battlefield to the severely battered Egyptians – who were thus able to claim a victory, albeit Pyrrhic – the Babylonian monarch conducted an orderly withdrawal into Palestine. After leaving troops in the garrison towns of Syria, he retired with the bulk of the army to Babylon in order to rest and regroup. In the wake of the temporary abandonment by the Babylonians of southern Palestine, the Egyptians followed up and invested the city of Gaza. That they failed to move further up the coast and exploit fully the Babylonian withdrawal suggests that the effort expended in halting the Babylonian advance into Egypt had been at such a cost that they no longer possessed the will or wherewithal to challenge Nebuchadnezzar on land. Indeed, the occupation of Gaza marks the final attempt of Egypt to gain control of the land area of the eastern Mediterranean seaboard. It has to be seen as a tacit acceptance of the reality of Babylonian domination and control.

From the perspective of Jerusalem, however, matters were seen in a much more optimistic light. The Babylonian withdrawal presaged the return of Egypt to Palestine and thus the dearest hopes of Jehoiakim and the majority of the political establishment of Judah were being realised. Deeming the retreat of Nebuchadnezzar to be final, Jehoiakim withheld his tribute to Babylon and was, therefore, in breach of his treaty with his overlord. It was an act that within three short years was to bring about his death and the deportation of the high and mighty of the land to Babylon. It was the direct cause of more than seventy years in exile for his people.

The Fall of Jerusalem

The failure of the Babylonian King to react directly against Judah in the year following Jehoiakim's rebellion must have been seen as a good sign to the Jews. However, Nebuchadnezzar returned to the Hatti-land in late 599 B.C. in order to deal with caravan raiders.

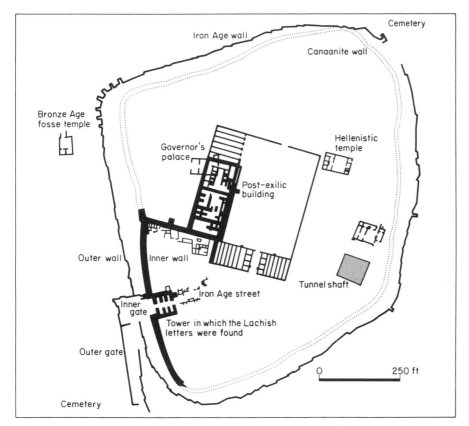

Once again it is interesting to note how similar were both the problems and the solutions faced by the Babylonians and the Assyrians before them. Less than fifty years earlier, Assurbanipal had sent units of the Assyrian army into the desert to destroy the tented settlements and plunder the waterholes of the Arabs. Nebuchadnezzar adopted an identical strategy. From the garrison bases of Carchemish, Riblah and Hamath, he despatched his own troops into the desert in an operation that would be described in the parlance of modern counter-insurgency warfare as a 'search and destroy' mission.

Seemingly at his leisure, Nebuchadnezzar invoked the terms of the treaties with his vassals and ordered them to attack and harrass the borders of Judah. In conjunction with auxiliary Babylonian forces based in southern Syria, the Aramaeans, Moabites and Ammonites began a campaign against Judah from the north and the east that must have done much to drain the military resources of the Jewish state. The continual raiding caused an influx into Jerusalem of people seeking safety. One such group were the Rechabites, the archetypal abstainers from the vine, whose descendants in 'spirit', are still with us.

In the following year, however, the Babylonian army itself moved against Judah. In all probability it was only a short time after the events of the year 597 B.C. that a scribe at the court of Nebuchadnezzar in Babylon

This reconstructed plan of Lachish, the fortified city to the south west of Jerusalem, is based upon archaeological excavation and thus shows several major periods of occupation. It is where the important Ostraca, the 'Lachish letters' were found.

was ordered to record the campaign. Preparing a small tablet of damp clay and taking up his *qan tuppi* or reed-stylus, he inscribed on it in cuneiform the formal account in the *Chronicle* of the operations against Al Yahudu, the city of Judah:

In the seventh year, in the month of Kislev, the Babylonian king mustered his troops, and having marched to the land of Hatti, besieged the city of Judah, and on the second day of the month of Adar took the city and captured the king. He appointed therein a king of his choice, received its heavy tribute and sent them to Babylon.

Capture of the City

The Bible has nothing to say about the seeming rapidity of the Babylonian advance on Jerusalem. Nebuchadnezzar had mustered his army in Babylon during the November of 598 B.C. and within a matter of three months had taken the city. There can be no doubt that the specific mention of Jerusalem, as 'the city of Judah', means that its reduction and capture was the main task of that year's operations in the west. Nebuchadnezzar was not a man to embark upon the task of laying siege to a city with defences as powerful as those of Jerusalem without very careful preparation. Over a century before, King Sennacherib had been frustrated in his efforts to take the city. The Assyrians, who had a justifiable reputation for ruthless efficiency when it came to siege warfare had to satisfy themselves with the destruction of the lesser fortress of Lachish. It is unlikely that in 597 B.C. the defences of Jerusalem were any less strong than when Sennacherib had laid siege. So why did it fall so rapidly?

The Babylonian army that moved against Jerusalem did so fully prepared for a long siege. No doubt Nebuchadnezzar had spent the time since Jehoiakim's revolt making careful preparations to punish his rebellious vassal. Knowledge of the city's defences would have been acquired and to this, intelligence would have been added that concerned the state of Judah's own army. Additionally, the attacks of the Ammonites, Moabites and Aramaeans over the preceding years may well have been part of a longer term strategy to 'bleed' the Judaean forces before he invaded. Little notice seems to have been taken of the possibility of Egyptian intervention.

Death of Jehoiakim

Ultimately, the explanation for the rapid fall of Jerusalem must be seen in terms of the changed political circumstances brought about by the death of Jehoiakim in December 598 B.C. However, different sources give conflicting accounts of the demise of this monarch. The *Second Book of Kings* (24:6) speaks of him dying a natural death.

On the other hand the *Second Book of Chronicles* (36:7) has a varying account of his fate: 'Nebuchadnezzar, king of Babylon attacked him, loaded him with chains and took him to Babylon'.

Nevertheless, it is accepted by most commentators that Jehoiakim died a natural death some three months before Jerusalem fell to Nebuchadnezzar and that he was succeeded by his son Jehoiakin.

It was not an enviable time for a young man to assume the mantle of kingship, and his reign was very short. On 15–16th March 597 B.C., in the company of his mother, his retinue, his nobles and his officials, he went out from the city and surrendered to Nebuchadnezzar.

We have no source that tells us why Jehoiakin felt it necessary to surrender. There is simply no way of corroborating the statement made by Flavius Josephus in his *Jewish Antiquities* to the effect that Nebuchadnezzar gained an entrance to Jerusalem by falsely promising Jehoiakin leniency, but then changed his mind and laid siege to the city.

Perhaps the Egyptians indicated that they were not prepared to help, and the arrival of Nebuchadnezzar in person finally brought the young king to the view that only by throwing himself on the mercy of the Babylonian monarch could Jerusalem be spared the horrors of a prolonged siege. Whatever the reason the *Second Book of Kings* states clearly that Jehoiakin: 'surrendered to the king of Babylon, and the king of Babylon took them prisoner in the eighth year of his reign.'

The gates of the great city were thrown open and the Babylonian troops entered to begin the task of assessing the spoil and booty to be taken back to Babylon.

The Lachish Ostraca. These drawings illustrate two of the shards of pottery excavated from the site of the main gate at Lachish, the fortified city to the south west of Jerusalem. On them, inscribed in Hebrew, is correspondence between two officers in the Judaean army concerning incidents occurring during the time of the Babylonian siege of Jerusalem.

Deportation

From amongst the population of Jerusalem, swollen by the many thousands who had fled to the city for safety in the face of the Babylonian advance, the officers of the Great King selected those who would be deported to Babylon. The description of the Babylonian treatment of Jerusalem found in the Bible well illustrates the price paid by the people of Judah for their ill-fated rebellion against their Babylonian overlord:

The latter [the Babylonians] carried off all the treasures of the temple of Yahweh and the treasures of the palace and broke up all the golden furnishings which Solomon the king had made for the sanctuary of Yahweh . . . He carried all Jerusalem off into exile, all the nobles and all the notables, ten thousand of these were exiled, with all the blacksmiths and metalworkers; only the poorest people in the country were left behind. He deported Jehoiakin to Babylon, as also the king's mother, his officials and the nobility of the country; he made them all leave Jerusalem for exile in Babylon. All the men of distinction, seven thousand of them, the blacksmiths and metalworkers, one thousand of them, all the men capable of bearing arms, were led off into exile in Babylon by the king of Babylon.

(2 Kings 24:13–16)

However, there is some uncertainty as to the exact number of deportees. Jeremiah gives a much smaller figure of three thousand and twenty three

Judaeans for the deportation of 597 B.C. Indeed he quotes figures for the two later deportations, in 586 and 581, that taken in addition to those he gives for the first deportation in 597 B.C. total less than one half of those spoken of in the *Book of Kings*.

Policy and Purpose

The Babylonian policy of dealing with recalcitrant vassals was, not surprisingly, very similar to that adopted by the Assyrians. The motives in either case stemmed from security considerations and economic gain.

In the case of the former, it was assumed that by deporting the leading elements of the population – the King, nobility, senior military figures and the temple priesthood – the defeated vassal was deprived of those in the country most likely to sponsor rebellion. A process of political decapitation rendered the kingdom much more amenable to the wishes of the overlord. In addition, the psychological blow of the deportations was sufficient to 'break the will' of those who were left and remove any desire to translate residual nationalist sentiment into further rebellion.

It would be wrong, however, to imagine the actual process of deportation as being like the 'death march' on Bataan in World War 2. Certainly, on the 'long trek' to Babylon, people must have died; but it seems this was a consequence more of the distance involved and the rigours of the climate than any deliberate policy of deprivation by the Babylonians. Indeed, bearing in mind that the deportees were seen by their conquerors as an economic resource, it is not surprising that considerable care was exercised in ensuring that as many prisoners as possible arrived in good condition.

The selection for deportation of artisans alongside the 'high and mighty' of the land demonstrates the way that Nebuchadnezzar intended to use the skills and expertise of Judaean blacksmiths and metalworkers. In being set to work in the great city, these craftsmen found themselves employing their expertise alongside others from Tyre, Sidon, Elam and Syria, who had like themselves been deported following the capture of their cities or who had been taken to Babylon as part of the annual tribute levied upon his vassals by Nebuchadnezzar. Their task was one of transforming Babylon into the greatest city in the world.

Great Babylon

Whilst the Kings of Assyria revelled in their imperial conquests and in the martial ardour of their armies, the Kings of Babylon, whilst no less committed to the imperial drive for conquest and expansion, left no lasting monuments as a testimony to their wars or the prowess of their arms. It is possible to wander through galleries in a number of the

world's major museums and gain a remarkable insight into the formidable instrument of aggrandisement that was the Assyrian army and gauge from the care taken over the rendering of even the smallest detail of military equipment that here was where the 'heart and treasure' of the Kings of Assyria lay. In stark contrast, it is only on the building bricks that litter Babylon that we perceive the real concerns of Nebuchadnezzar and his successors.

Designating himself the: 'Provider of Esagila and Ezida', Nebuchadnezzar tells us that his pride lay in his service to the gods and in the provision of fine cities within which they might dwell. It was in his building achievements that Nebuchadnezzar seems to have gained his greatest satisfaction. His expansionist policy cannot be seen as distinct from the task of rebuilding Babylon; it was a matter intimately related to his ability to achieve that policy. Indeed, even a century and more after his death Herodotus could say of his labour that Babylon 'surpasses in splendour any city of the known world'. The imperial policy and his frequent campaigns in the west were unambiguously directed by Nebuchadnezzar towards acquisition of booty and manpower that could be used in the building work in Babylon. The rationale for the deportation policy shows how carefully Babylonian officers set about rounding up artisans with specific skills. This was no arbitrary policy but one conceived with distinct building needs in Babylon in mind. This underlying purpose of the Babylonian King was an essential part of his conquests, as in the 'liberation' of the 'hardy, tall, stout cedars of the Lebanon' and the evident satisfaction he expressed that they would be employed in the service of 'Marduk my king'. In this case they were

A small section from the Lachish wall relief depicting the Assyrian King Sennacherib's siege of that city in 705 B.C. It shows a group of Judaean prisoners beginning the long march into exile. The deportations carried out by the Babylonians over a century later would have looked little different.

31

plainly destined to be used in the refurbishment of the roofing and gates of the shrines of the major gods of Babylon. Whilst space is not available here to give a fully detailed history and description of Babylon itself, an account of the rebuilding of Babylon by Nebuchadnezzar tells us something of the man himself and so requires some insight, however small, into the object of his labours.

The City

At the time of Nebuchadnezzar the city of Babylon was bisected by the River Euphrates. On the eastern bank lay what was called the 'old city'. The walls which enclosed this area were rather more than a mile long and formed an irregular square within which were the most important buildings. It is this part of the city that has received the greatest attention from the archaeologists. Whilst it is known that Nebuchadnezzar extended the walls westwards to embrace the settlement on the other bank, little is actually known in detail concerning this part of the city as much of it is now underneath the present bed of the Euphrates, the course of which has moved westward since Neo-Babylonian times.

Defensive Walls

Two sets of fortifications enclosed the city. The inner fortifications are those referred to already as enclosing the 'old city' and the settlement on the western bank. The outer city wall was begun by Nabopolassar and completed by his son, but only covered the eastern bank. Together they formed a formidable defensive system of considerable complexity.

The Inner Wall was in reality two walls, one within the other. The 'inner wall' had a thickness of 21 feet and was higher than the 'outer' wall, whose thickness was about 12 feet. They were separated by a space of 24 feet filled with earth. On top was constructed a military roadway, at parapet level and wide enough (according to Herodotus) to allow a four-horse chariot to pass. Both of these walls had crenellated battlements and at intervals along the walls were towers. On the inner part of the wall they were spaced every 59 feet whilst on the outer part of the wall and at a lower level they were spaced every 67 feet. Outside of this Inner Wall was an encircling moat constructed on the inner face of strong kiln-baked bricks set in bitumin. The source of the water for this canal was, of course, the Euphrates itself. Built into the Inner Wall were nine gates named after the gods of the city, of which the most famous was the Ishtar Gate named for the goddess of love. Clearly these gates opened out onto bridges that crossed the canal and provision must have been made when they were built to allow them to be raised or dealt with by some other means in the event of a siege. Each gate itself was very heavily fortified and the massive programme was embarked upon: 'In order to strengthen the defences of Esagila that the evil and the wicked might not oppress Babylon.'

In the month of Nisan, Babylon celebrated the great New Year religious festival during which Nebuchadnezzar grasped the hand of his lord Marduk and escorted statues of the gods beyond the city walls to the Akitu House.

The Outer Wall was also a double wall which began a mile-and-a-half to the north of the Ishtar Gate on the east bank. It ran south-easterly to a point roughly parallel with the Temple of Esagila in the 'old city'. It then turned south-westwards to meet the Euphrates a quarter of a mile south of the defensive inner system. In total, these two great walls embraced an area of some 850 hectares and could contain up to 200,000 men.

An artist's impression of the appearance of the inner fortifications of Babylon on the western side of the city. Clearly shown are the crenellated fortifications designed to withstand prolonged siege. The picture conveys a powerful image of the strength of Babylon's defences.

Temples and Ziggurats

Nabopolassar and Nebuchadnezzar both expended much time and wealth in the refurbishment of the temples that made Babylon so important as a religious cult centre.

Of the many temples and other religious buildings in a city in which there were hundreds of shrines, two in particular are outstanding; the great ziggurat of Entemenanki and the temple complex of Esagila.

At the time Nabopolassar and his son set to work to rebuild the ziggurat it still exhibited the great damage caused to it by Sennacherib's destruction of much of the city in 689 B.C. Entemenanki, 'the building which is the Foundation of Heaven and Earth', took many years to rebuild. The completed ziggurat rose to a height of nearly 300 feet and dominated the view of the city. Its base at its maximum extent was a square with sides of about 300 feet. The main mass of the ziggurat was composed of trodden clay although the outer casing was composed of burnt brick nearly 50 feet thick. The first and second levels were reached by a staircase about 30 feet wide although the appearance of the upper storeys is uncertain and artists' reconstructions are at best tentative.

An immense labour was required to rebuild the ziggurat and many men deported to Babylon were employed on it. Nebuchadnezzar mentions that a number of kings exiled in the city, including Jehoiakin, were made to symbolically carry a corvée basket at the foundation ceremony.

The small building which topped the ziggurat and which was the 'dwelling place' of Marduk was faced by blue enamelled bricks which caused the topmost stage 'to shine like the heavens themselves'. The completion of the rebuilding of Entemenanki was a time of great festivity and rejoicing.

In August–September 587 B.C., Jerusalem fell to Nebuchadnezzar's army after a two-year siege. Deportation and systematic destruction left the city a devastated and desolate ruin.

A model showing the great ziggurat of Entemenanki or 'The Foundation of Heaven and Earth'. It was rebuilt by Nabopolassar and his son Nebuchadnezzar, following its virtual destruction by the Assyrian King Sennacherib during his sack of Babylon in 689 B.C.

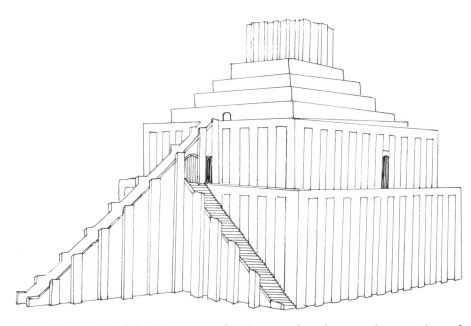

An artist's impression – tentative because of the lack of definitive evidence – of the great ziggurat of Entemananki.

To the south of the Entemenanki ziggurat lay the temple complex of Esagila or 'the Temple of the Raised Head'. The temple of Esagila was devoted to Marduk although the main temple of Nabu and Marduk's consort, Sarpanitum – 'The Shining One' were also to be found therein.

The main shrine of Marduk, otherwise known as 'Bel' or 'The Lord' was a chamber whose interior was completely overlain with gold. Within the shrine was a large golden image of Marduk and Sarpanitum, and other images who flanked the divine couple and tended to their needs. Kurub, or winged statues, guarded the entrance to the chamber whose interior was seen only by the priests of the deities and the King.

Palaces

At the time of Nebuchadnezzar there were three principal palaces known as the Northern, Southern and Summer palaces. Of these, it was the southern palace that was the most important. A very extensive building, it functioned not just as a royal residence but also as an administrative centre. The design was built around five courtyards, each one used by the King's secretariat, and included the King's private rooms, the state rooms, the garrison and the harem. In the north-eastern part of this palace the archaeologists came upon a structure that may well have been the famous Hanging Gardens of Babylon. In the vaulted chambers that underpinned this structure tablets listing the issue of grain and oil mention the name of Jehoiakin of Judah.

The Processional Way

The most famous of the many streets of Babylon was the Processional Way. Running along the eastern side of the Southern palace it was onto

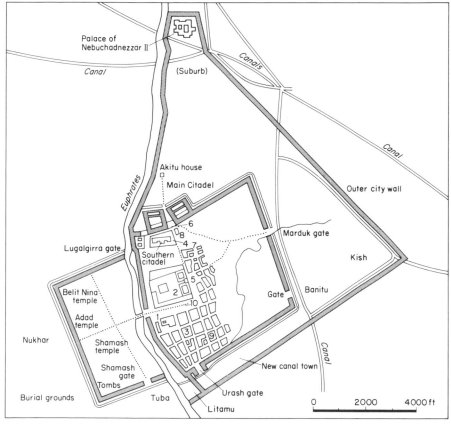

A plan view of Babylon under Nebuchadnezzar, in the sixth century B.C., showing the major work of construction undertaken by him and his father Nabopolassar.

1. Esagila
2. Entemenanki (ziggurat)
3. Temple of Gula
4. Hanging gardens
5. Holy gate
6. Ishtar gate
7. Temple of Ishtar
8. Temple of Ninmakh
9. Temple of Ninurta
10. Processional way

A modern reproduction of the Ishtar Gate built at Babylon by the Iraqi Department of Antiquities. Like its German counterpart, which is located at the Voderasiatisches Museum in Berlin, this is not a full-size replica. The original was wide enough to allow the passage of heavy, four-horsed chariots.

the Processional Way that the statues of Marduk and the other gods were brought out from Esagila to be borne through the magnificent Ishtar Gate to the Akitu House at the time of the New Year Festival. Approaching Babylon from the north via the Ishtar Gate one would pass along the Processional Way between high walls. Each wall was lined with the figures of lions moulded in glazed brick. On the road surface itself Nebuchadnezzar laid large limestone flags flanked by slabs of red breccia veined with white.

The Ishtar Gate itself was double, running the width of both fortification walls. The gate was decorated with glazed tiles depicting 150 bulls and Sirrush dragons. The colour of the background tiles was a very vivid blue with the bulls and dragons appearing alternately in white and yellow.

Even this very short description of Babylon communicates something of the magnificence of the city in the time of Nebuchadnezzar. Perhaps then we can understand the words attributed to the Great King himself:

Great Babylon! Was it not built by me as a royal residence by the force of my might and for the majesty of my glory

(Daniel 4:27)

Twenty-three centuries later the product of such great labour is slowly being reclaimed from the earth that 'swallowed' it up. In the ruins

36

uncovered by the careful and diligent work of the archaeologists, it is still possible to discern the greatness of Babylon and sense the power and majesty of its greatest architect and builder.

A King of His Own Choice

Nebuchadnezzar was able to maintain his new realms whilst Babylon flourished. In the place of Jehoiakin, who was to spend the rest of his days in exile, Nebuchadnezzar chose the youngest son of Josiah, the former king. However, to demonstate that his elevation to the kingship of Judah was in the gift of the King of Babylon, Nebuchadnezzar had the successor's name changed from Mattaniah to Zedekiah, which means 'Yahweh-is-my-justice'. It was chosen to symbolize that, in taking his oath of fealty to his overlord, Zedekiah had called upon Yahweh to witness his declaration of loyalty.

The gods of Babylon had also been invoked to witness that Zedekiah had declared to Nebuchadnezzar that he would 'surely keep the country for him and attempt no uprising nor show friendliness to the Egyptians'. The final part of the vassal treaty required a recital of the ritual curses that would be invoked if Zedekiah broke the terms of the treaty.

However, the harsh punishment that would inevitably fall on the head of the Judaean King and his people was no arbitrary destruction exercised by an aggrieved monarch. Rather, the gods of Babylon and the God of

A close-up of one of the many bulls depicted on the Ishtar Gate and whose glazed finish of yellow alternating with white, on a vivid blue background, caused the whole edifice to blaze in the sunlight. The other creature to appear on the Gate was the mythological Sirrush dragon. A hybrid creature with the head and horns of the Arabian viper, front legs of a cat and the rear of a bird of prey, the tip of its tail has a scorpion's sting.

Judah, seeing the treaty broken by the very supplicant who had called upon them to witness his profession of loyalty, would demand vengeance upon him and would call upon the King of Babylon to be at once their arbiter and also the instrument of their punishment. It was because Zedekiah was Nebuchadnezzar's man on the throne of Judah that any future rebellion would be suppressed with harshness so severe that the continued existence of the throne of David was in danger.

Zedekiah's Weakness

It was a tragedy for Judah that Nebuchadnezzar's 'king of his own choosing' was so ill equipped for the task. Jehoiakim had been a headstrong, arrogant ruler but Zedekiah was from a different mould. A weak, mild-mannered and vacillating man, his self-confidence was undermined almost from the beginning by his realization that many in Judah still regarded Jehoiachin as the legitimate ruler of the land. In the end it was his own character defects and weaknesses that led directly to the débâcle of 587 B.C. with many in opposition to the will of Nebuchadnezzar.

As was his custom Nebuchadnezzar returned quickly to Babylon following the conclusion of the Judaean campaign. He had left behind him a people dazed and bewildered by the events of the previous few months. From within the context of their religious ideology, the unthinkable had happened: Jerusalem the inviolable had indeed been violated. How was this to be explained when Yahweh's temple, the sanctuary of the Lord, itself gave protection to Jerusalem?

Seeds of Defiance

In 593 B.C. the accession of Psammetichus II to the throne of Egypt led to a revival amongst the pro-Egyptian leadership in Judah who hoped that the new Pharaoh intended to challenge Babylonian control in Palestine. In anticipation, the rulers of Edom, Ammon, Moab, Tyre and Sidon sent their representatives to a conclave in Jerusalem to discuss the formation of an anti-Babylonian alliance. It was then that Jeremiah, in accord with the wishes of his God, picketed the meeting and having donned thongs and yokes, the symbols of submission, called on the assembled representatives to forgo their plans for rebellion.

In one of the personal and secret meetings that the prophet had with the King, he repeated the same message: rebellion was doomed to failure; it was Yahweh who had ordered that events be so; how could he therefore even contemplate rebellion knowing what he did?

Zedekiah displayed great indecision in response. Then, two events occurred that led the anti-Babylon faction to press ahead with plans to rebel. Pharaoh Psammetichus led a successful campaign into Nubia and in 591 B.C. made an expedition to Palestine, ostensibly for religious reasons. Following so soon after his triumph of arms in the south, the

event must have been interpreted as more than just a symbolic re-assertion of traditional Egyptian claims in the area. The failure of Nebuchadnezzar to make any appearance in Syria–Palestine since 594 B.C. must also have led some to interpret this as a sign of growing Babylonian weakness. To many in Judah the time seemed right to throw off the yoke of Babylon.

The End of Judah

The Bible itself has nothing to say concerning the reasons for Zedekiah's rebellion against Nebuchadnezzar. Nevertheless, one must conclude that he had been given cause to believe that Egyptian help would be forthcoming to counter the inevitable Babylonian response. It is only in this light that any sense can be made of his decision to declare formally his state of rebellion by withholding payment of tribute. The prophet Ezekiel alluded to this by making reference to the faithlessness of Zedekiah, who in breaking his oath to Nebuchadnezzar forgot that he had invoked the name of Yahweh, his God, to witness his profession of loyalty to the Babylonian monarch.

The date of the rebellion cannot be fixed with any certainty although it seems likely that Zedekiah was in violation of his oath of submission to his overlord by at least 589 B.C. Whatever, the response of

This small section of the Babylonian Chronicle records in cuneiform, the account of Nebuchadnezzar's taking of the city of Jerusalem in 597 B.C. Mentioned is the deportation of Jehoiakin and the installation of Zedekiah, 'the King of his own choice', as the new ruler of Judah.

Nebuchadnezzar was swift and harsh. In 588, the Babylonian army entered Judah bringing fire and destruction to the land, intent on just retribution for the rebellion of the vassal state. The doom of the kingdom and the end of the throne of David, which had so long been prophesied by Jeremiah, were at last at hand.

Under Siege

The Babylonian army moved rapidly to invest Jerusalem itself. In a manner reminiscent of the Assyrian campaign against Judah in 701 B.C., the Babylonians surrounded the city with a ring of extensive earthworks to enclose the population in order to prevent their coming or their going. Plainly, their intended strategy was to starve the city into surrender.

From the wall of the city, Zedekiah would have looked down upon the enemy soldiers struggling hard in the hot sun to throw up the earthworks. Already the familiar view beyond the city would be changing as the hordes of Babylonian troops cut down every available tree to underpin the great earth ramps that formed part of the surrounding ring. The horrors of siege warfare were a contemporary fact of life, but to the King and others contemplating the labour of the Babylonians, the first doubts as to the wisdom of their actions must have begun to enter their minds. In the great Temple of Solomon the daily sacrifices and rituals continued, but now there was an added sense of urgency in the supplications of the priests in their prayers to Yahweh. But Zedekiah already knew from the mouth of Jeremiah that Yahweh was deaf to the prayers of the people, oblivious to the sacrifices made in his name.

With the city fully invested, a token force of soldiers was left to guard the perimeter while the bulk of the army moved out into the highlands of Judah to begin a campaign designed to devastate the entire country. One by one, the towns of the land were subjected to fire and destruction. From Gibeah in the north to Arad in the south, and from Eglon in the west to En-Gedi in the east, the Babylonian army systematically set about destroying the major settlements of Judah. The archaeological record well attests to the savagery of the Babylonian onslaught.

From his base at Riblah, Nebuchadnezzar received regular reports from his senior commanders in the field concerning the progress of the campaign. Unlike the short siege of 597 B.C., he was not present at all during the second siege. The position of Riblah, with its good communications to the south, allowed him to be informed rapidly of events in Judah whilst overseeing the continued operations in the thirteen-year-long siege of Tyre. It was here that he received news of the advance along the coast of an Egyptian army towards Gaza.

It seems that only after Zedekiah made a direct appeal to Apries, the new Pharaoh of Egypt, was help from this quarter forthcoming. Among a number of messages scribbled on potsherds (discovered near the gate of the fortress of Lachish during the excavations of the Wellcome–Marston expedition in the 1930s) there is one that refers to the despatch to Egypt of a General Konyahu, son of Elnatan. It is possible that Konyahu was the head of the military delegation sent by Zedekiah to Apries to request Egyptian military help. The force despatched by the Pharaoh gave, at best, a temporary respite to those besieged in Jerusalem. The Babylonian forces surrounding the city temporarily abandoned the siege lines and deployed for battle against the Egyptian forces in the area of Gaza. Whether or not the two opposing armies met in battle is uncertain. What is clear, however, is that the Egyptian army withdrew again into Egypt after tentative probings. Thereafter, no Egyptian aid was forthcoming. Patently, Pharaoh Apries had abandoned Judah to its fate.

Prophesy of Doom
The withdrawal of the Babylonian army to deal with the Egyptian incursion seemed to many in Jerusalem to be a hopeful sign. Zedekiah sent a delegation to the prophet Jeremiah with the request that he intercede with Yahweh to save the city. But Jeremiah had no words of balm or hope for the King, only the same message of unrelenting doom.

The respite gained by the Babylonian withdrawal provided the opportunity to ease the desperate food situation. This could have been no easy task as the Babylonian army itself was living off the land. Even in those areas that had been spared from the 'scorched earth' campaign of the

The ruins of Nebuchadnezzar's great palace in Babylon, known to the German archaeological team who excavated it as the 'Southern Citadel'.

Babylonian soldiery, the available supplies would have gone first to serve the needs of the army. Those Judaeans in the countryside who had survived the initial Babylonian onslaught must have been living in the most desperate of circumstances.

It was also during this interregnum that Jeremiah, while preparing to leave the city, was arrested on the grounds that he was deserting to the enemy. There were many amongst the King's retinue who wanted Jeremiah executed as his continual pronouncements of Jerusalem's fall were undermining morale amongst the soldiers and the people. The weak and vacillating monarch, a puppet of his advisers, handed the prophet over with a comment that provides an insight into the true state of affairs within the Judaean court: 'He is in your hands as you know, for the King is powerless to oppose you'. So taking Jeremiah they lowered him into the cistern of the King's son Malchiah and left him to die. He was rescued by an Ethiopian servant of Zedekiah who had appealed to the King to allow him to save the prophet. Jeremiah was then taken to the Court of the Guard for safe keeping. It was while he was here that Zedekiah summoned Jeremiah for a secret meeting in the Temple.

In what was undoubtedly their last face-to-face meeting, Jeremiah tried to convince the King that even now, by throwing himself on the mercy of Nebuchadnezzar, his life and the city could be saved. However the King could only see things in terms of his own fear, afraid of his fate at the hands of those of his countrymen who had gone over to the Babylonian monarch if he surrendered. In the pathos of the moment Jeremiah told the King: 'You will not be handed over to them'.

Pleading with Zedekiah, Jeremiah then proceeded to tell him;

Please listen to Yahweh's voice as I have relayed it to you, and then all will go well with you and your life will be safe. But if you refuse to surrender, this is what Yahweh has shown me: the sight of all the women left in the king of Judah's palace being led off to the king of Babylon's generals . . . Yes, all your wives and children will be lead off to the Chaldeans, and you yourself will not escape their clutches but will be a prisoner in the clutches of the king of Babylon. As for this city, it will be burnt down.

(Jeremiah 38:20–23)

Zedekiah could not bring himself to do what the prophet asked and commanding Jeremiah to remain silent returned to his palace. But by that time the Babylonian army had returned and were taking the steps to bring the siege of Jerusalem to its bloody and desperate conclusion.

The Final Act

With the return of the Babylonian army, only Jerusalem and the fortified cities of Azekah and Lachish remained.

Azekah and Lachish both fell shortly after the Babylonian army resumed its siege of the capital. However, in the case of Lachish it is obvious from the archaeological record that its taking was no easy matter. The ferocity of the attack was such that fires set up against the city walls were so intense that the effect was startling:

masonry, consolidated into a chalky white mass streaked with red, had flowed in a liquid stream over the burnt road surface and lower wall, below which were piled charred heaps of burnt timber. In the angle below the north wall of the Bastion and the west revetment, breaches had been hurriedly repaired and any material available were forced again; indeed, evidence of destruction by fire was not difficult to find anywhere within the walls of the city.

(O. Tufnell)

The stage was now set for the final act itself – the capture of Jerusalem.

A much closer siege wall was set up by the Babylonians allowing the large siege towers that had been erected to be moved closer to the walls of Jerusalem. From these great towers, archers poured a withering fire of arrows down on to the heads of the defenders on the city walls. Below, rams proceeded to batter away at the stonework. The attack itself was concentrated on the northern wall. Certainly, the western wall of the city seems to have been too well constructed to allow the Babylonians to effect a breach.

In the fourth month of the eleventh year of Zedekiah, June–July of 587 B.C., the Babylonians breached the wall and broke into the city. For the defenders and others crowding within its walls, conditions were by now desperate. Hunger was by now gripping the city with the non-combatant population suffering the worst of the privation and what little food there was going to the soldiers. The *Book of Lamentations* paints vivid pictures of the horror of the siege for the people of Jerusalem:

The tongue of the baby at the breast,
stick to its palate for thirst;
little children ask for bread,
no one gives them any.
Those who used to eat only the best,
now lie dying in the streets;
those who were reared in the purple
claw at the rubbish heaps,
With their own hands, kindly women
cooked their own children,
this was their food,
Happier those killed by the sword,
than those killed by famine

The Babylonians penetrated the outer wall built by King Hezekiah over a century before. Once inside Jerusalem it was only a matter of time before the 'inner city', containing the palace and great temple within the walls built during the early period of the monarchy, succumbed.

With the Babylonians inside the city walls Zedekiah made the decision to flee the city. Infiltrating the Babylonian siege lines, the Judaean forces passed into the valley of the River Jordan known as the Arabeh and headed towards Ammon, the only other state that had stood by Zedekiah in his rebellion against Nebuchadnezzar.

The king then made his escape under cover of dark, with all the fighting men, by way of the gate between the two walls, which is near the king's garden – the Chaldeans had surrounded the city and made his way towards the Arabeh

It was a forlorn hope. The Babylonians, learning of the escape, pursued the fleeing Judaeans and captured Zedekiah in the plains of Jericho. By this time he was alone, except for possibly a few of his retinue, his troops having deserted and run for their lives. A sad, pathetic and lonely figure he was placed in chains and taken to Riblah, there to face Nebuchadnezzar in the certain knowledge that this time there would be no mercy.

Judgement of the King

At Riblah, as Jeremiah had foretold, Zedekiah was brought to Nebuchadnezzar and was condemned by the very terms of the vassal treaty he had acceded to in 597 B.C. and had invoked Yahweh to witness. A shattered man, he had to stand in the presence of the Babylonian King and watch as one by one his sons were brought in and slaughtered before his eyes.

These tragic images were the last to be inscribed on Zedekiah's memory. Almost immediately after, and in accord with the judgement of Nebuchadnezzar, burning irons put out his eyes. Dragged from the chamber, blinded and stumbling, he was loaded onto a cart and taken to Babylon, there to disappear from sight and from the pages of history into one of the dungeons of the Babylonian King.

The Sack of Zion

Following the surrender of the city, which must have occurred shortly after Zedekiah's capture, Nebuchadnezzar sent Nebuzaradan, the commander of his guard, from Riblah to oversee the systematic sacking and destruction of Jerusalem.

The Temple of Solomon was burned down and all the items of value, of gold, silver and bronze, within it were taken off to Babylon as booty. The royal palace which was part of the same complex of buildings as the temple suffered the same fate. The Babylonian objective was to ensure that no buildings suitable as strong defensive points were left standing. From the temple mount, the soldiery moved down into the city itself demolishing and burning all the 'great houses' belonging to the nobility, destroying any building that could serve as a potential point of resistance. Finally, the walls themselves were pulled down. Over a century later, in 446 B.C. Nehemiah, returning to the city was able to say 'Jerusalem is in ruins and its gates burnt down'.

Babylonian destruction of the city and of all the major towns and cities of the land had been such that for those survivors not deported, existence was in all probability reduced to a subsistence level. These poor people were left behind to tend the vineyards and to plough the land – but the kingdom of Judah, which had survived for some four hundred years from the time of David, was ended.

Just inside the city walls of Babylon, by the Ishtar Gate, are these ruins of the temple dedicated to the god Ninmakh.

Legacy of Exile

Nebuchadnezzar died in 562 B.C. after a reign of forty-two years. His son and successor Amel-Marduk released Jehoiakin from his imprisonment and had him eat from the royal table.

The majority of Jewish captives were settled in communities alongside the Chebar River. Unlike the Assyrians, who did everything possible to break down the national identity of their deported populations, the Babylonians allowed the Jews and others to retain their distinctive religious and national identities. Many found the experience of exile from the pleasant land very difficult to come to terms with:

> *By the rivers of Babylon*
> *we sat and wept*
> *at the memory of Zion.*
> *On the poplars there*
> *we had hung our harps*
> *For there our gaolers had asked us*
> *to sing them a song,*
> *our captors to make merry,*
> *'Sing us a song of Zion'*
> *How could we sing a song of Yahweh*
> *on alien soil?*
>
> (Psalms 137:1–4)

It was here, in the absence of the Temple, that the first meeting places or synagogues were established in order that the scriptures could be read. It was a great period of activity for the Jewish people; old traditions were rethought and rewritten. Out of the experience of the exile, a new insight into the faith of their fathers was born.

When the Jewish exiles were at last allowed to return home, by permission of the Persians, the new masters of Babylon, they carried with them ideas and thoughts that would change the world.

For many, the enduring symbol of Babylon is the basalt lion, first uncovered by Arab villagers in 1776. Shown mauling a victim, the sculpture was apparently unfinished.

46

Chronology of Events

627 B.C. Death of Assurbanipal, King of Assyria. Accession to throne of Ashur-etil-ilani.

626 B.C. Nabopolassar seizes power in Babylon; in November is crowned King of Akkad. Civil war in Assyrian Empire when Sin-shar-ishkun (other son of Assurbanipal) challenges his brother for the throne of Assyria.

625 B.C. Cyaxares, King of Media defeats the Scythians, rulers of the Medes since around 652 B.C. Nabopolassar begins diplomatic overtures to Medes for joint military action against Assyria.

623 B.C. Sin-shar-ishkun secures Assyrian throne. Remains King until his death in 612 B.C..

620 B.C. First mention of Nebuchadnezzar as eldest son of Nabopolassar in connection with rebuilding ziggurat of Entemenanki in Babylon.

616 B.C. Nabopolassar begins operations against Assyrians, who are supported by Egyptian forces.

614 B.C. Medes and Babylonians sack Assur. Alliance between Cyaxares of Media and Nabopolassar concluded. Sealed by marriage of Nebuchadnezzar to Amytis, daughter of Median king.

612 B.C. Fall of Nineveh. Rump of Assyrian army retreats to Harran. Ashur-ubalit crowned last King of Assyria.

610 B.C. Medes and Babylonians sack Harran. Nebuchadnezzar assumes first military command.

609 B.C. Pharaoh Necho II gives full-scale support to remnants of Assyrian forces. Taking his army into Syria defeats army of Judah and kills King Josiah at Megiddo. Deprives Jehoahaz of Judah's throne and makes Jehoiakim King in his place.

607 B.C. Nebuchadnezzar undertakes first independent campaign as army commander.

605 B.C. As Crown Prince, Nebuchadnezzar assumes full command of Babylonian army in Syria. Decisively defeats Necho II at Battle of Carchemish.

604 B.C. Nebuchadnezzar marches into Palestine. Takes city of Ashkelon after siege and receives submission of Jehoiakim, who becomes vassal of Babylon.

600 B.C. Jehoiakim rebels against Nebuchadnezzar by failing to render tribute.

598 B.C. Jehoiakim dies; succeeded by his son Jehoiakin.

597 B.C. Nebuchadnezzar invades Judah. Jehoiakin surrenders and with many other Judaeans is deported to Babylon. Nebuchadnezzar chooses Mattaniah, uncle of Jehoiakin, as Judah's new King. Changes his name to Zedekiah.

590 B.C. Zedekiah rebels against Nebuchadnezzar.

588 B.C. Nebuchadnezzar invades Judah and lays siege to Jerusalem.

587 B.C. Jerusalem falls to Babylonian army. Zedekiah blinded and sent to Babylon, where he dies in captivity. Jerusalem sacked and population deported.

585 B.C. Babylonian mediation ends Lydian–Median territorial dispute in Anatolia.

581 B.C. Third Babylonian deportation of persons from Judah.

573 B.C. Tyre surrenders to Babylon after thirteen-year siege.

567 B.C. Possible Babylonian invasion of Egypt.

562 B.C. Death of Nebuchadnezzar in the forty-second year of his reign.

Bibliography

Ackroyd, P.R. *Israel under Babylon and Persia* Oxford University Press, 1986

Anderson, B.W. *The Living World of the Old Testament* Longman, 1966

Beek, M.A. *Atlas of Mesopotamia* Nelson, 1962

Bright, J.A. *History of Israel* SCM, 1981

Edwards, I.E.S. (ed) *Cambridge Ancient History* Vol III, 2 & 3, Cambridge University Press, 1975

Finegan, J. *Archaeological History of the Ancient Middle East,* Dorset, 1986

Grant, M. *The Ancient Mediterranean* Weidenfeld & Nicolson, 1969

Grant, M. *The History of Ancient Israel* Weidenfeld & Nicolson, 1984

Herodotus *The Histories* Penguin, 1986

Kenyon, K. (Revised Moorey, P.R.S.), *The Bible and Recent Archaeology* British Museum Publications, 1987

Lloyd, S. *The Archaeology of Mesopotamia,* Thames and Hudson, 1984

Miller, J.M. and Hayes, J.H. *A History of Ancient Israel and Judah* SCM, 1986

Oates, J. *Babylon* Thames and Hudson, 1986

Pritchard, J.B. (Ed) *The Ancient Near East,* Vols 1 & 2, Princeton, 1958 & 1975

Roux, G. *Ancient Iraq* Pelican, 1964

Saggs, H.W.F. *The Greatness that was Babylon* Sidgwick & Jackson, 1962

Saggs, H.W.F. *The Might that was Assyria* Sidgwick & Jackson, 1984

Walker, C.B.F. *Cuneiform* British Museum Publications, 1987

Winton-Thomas, D. (Ed) *Documents from Old Testament Times* Nelson, 1958

Wiseman, D.J. *Nebuchadnezzar and Babylon* Oxford University Press, 1983

Index

Page numbers in *italics* refer to illustrations.

Illustrations
Colour plates by Richard Hook
Line illustrations by Chesca Potter and Suzie Hole
Maps and diagrams by Chartwell Illustrators
Photographs courtesy of: Directorate of Antiquities and Heritage, Baghdad (pages 15, 19, 33, 34 and 36); Iraqi Cultural Centre, London (pages 41, 45 and 46); Trustees of the British Museum (pages 31 and 39); Voderasiatisches Museum, Berlin/Christo Bagell (page 37)